The Secret Life of
BUGS, BEES, & TREES

happy yak

CONTENTS

A MESSAGE FROM LUNA 4

WHEN LUNA WAS BORN 6

ALL ABOUT INSECTS 8

HOW THE BUTTERFLIES GOT THEIR COLOR
A bug tale from North America 10

HOME SWEET HOME 12

NIGHTTIME BUGS 14

BUG BUILDERS 16

THE SONG OF THE CICADA
A bug tale from Ancient Greece 18

SWIMMING BUGS 20

NOISY BUGS 22

HOW THE RACE WAS WON
A story from Brazil 24

GIANT FRIENDS 26

THE TINIEST BUGS 28

WHAT WE SEE 30

MOST AMAZING 32

WHY THE ANTS CAN NEVER WIN
A story from South Africa 34

THE GRUESOME GANG 36

FIGHT BACK! 38

ACTING STARS 40

THE WORLD NEEDS BUGS! 42

BE A LADYBUG FRIEND 44

A MESSAGE FROM BUZZWING 46

WHEN BUZZWING WAS BORN 48

ALL ABOUT BEES 50

THE BABY AND THE BEES
A bee tale from Greece 52

A HAPPY HIVE HOME 54

COME INSIDE 56

THE LADY OF THE MOON
A story from Australia 58

BRILLIANT BEE DANCE 60

FLY THE MEADOW 62

FLY AWAY, BEES 64

SUMMER SWEET 66

THE BOY WHO ATE SKY HONEY
A bee tale from India 68

BUZZING AROUND THE WORLD 70

HONEY THIEVES 72

CHEE-CHEE, COME WITH ME 74

HIDEY-HOLE HOMES 76

HOW THE ELEPHANTS GOT THEIR TRUNKS
A bee tale from Thailand 78

CITY BEES 80

THE BEEKEEPER COMES 82

WINTER SNUGGLE-UP 84

BE A BEE FRIEND 86

A MESSAGE FROM OAKHEART 88

WHEN OAKHEART WAS BORN 90

HOW TO FEED A TREE 92

MAGIC IN THE FOREST
A tree tale from Britain 94

WONDROUS FORESTS OF THE WORLD 96

HOW OAKHEART GREW 98
ROUGH AND WRINKLY 100
SECRETS INSIDE US 102
TREE-TALKING 104
ENEMIES! 106
TALLEST, OLDEST, BIGGEST, WIDEST 108
THE WOODS IN SPRING 110
THE FAIRY TREE
A tree tale from Scotland 112
THE WOODS IN SUMMER 114
THE SUMMER STORM
A tree tale from Norway 116
THE WOODS IN AUTUMN 118
THE TREE OF LIFE
A tree tale from Persia 120
THE WOODS IN WINTER 122
TREES MADE THESE 124
HOW TO BE TREE-HAPPY 126

I'm like a shiny bead with spots,
sitting on your flowerpots.
I fly around on tiny wings
and love the warmth that sunshine brings.
I'm Luna the ladybug. Hello!
I'll help you meet some bugs. Let's go!

Dear Reader,

I'm here to take you on a journey through the world of insects (we are often nicknamed bugs, too). Together we'll find out about the biggest and tiniest insects, the nighttime insects, and the noisy insects. We'll be discovering the cleverest builders, swimmers, and flyers.

I'll be telling you some stories from long ago and from around the world, too. Butterflies, grasshoppers, bees, and ants are all waiting to share their tales with you.

Oh, and look out for my teeny-tiny bug facts along the way.

Are you ready? OK! Let's see what we can find among the flowers and leaves.

Luna the ladybug

WHEN LUNA WAS BORN
Tiny eggs and big changes

At the very beginning of summer last year, I was just a tiny egg. I was laid along with a cluster of other eggs on the underside of a leaf.

My egg was yellow and lemon-shaped.

An aphid. Yum!

I grew to about ½ inch long.

½ inch

After a few days I hatched out, but I didn't look like a ladybug yet. I was black and spiky with orange stripes—a larva! Most insects are larva when they first hatch, though they might look different to me. When I was a larva, I spent my time eating all the plant-eating bugs—called aphids—that I could find.

I grew quickly because of all those aphid snacks. A couple of times I got so big that my skin grew too tight, so I shed it and grew a new one. After about 3 weeks I glued myself to a leaf and turned into a little spotted blob called a pupa.

Pupa

Inside my pupa an incredible thing happened. My body changed completely! It's called metamorphosis (met-a-more-foh-sis). It happens to lots of insects. After a week or so I emerged as a pale-colored ladybug, but I soon turned red and my black spots appeared.

I'm me at last!

TEENY-TINY BUG FACT
There are more than 5,000 different types of ladybug in the world. We are lots of different colors and we have different numbers of spots.

Ladybugs are a type of beetle. I am a seven-spotted ladybird.

ALL ABOUT INSECTS
Legs, wings and other things

Insects come in lots of different shapes and sizes, but we all have some body parts that are similar.

Mouthparts—I use mine to chew up aphids.

Tiny **claws**

Two **antennae** that help us to smell, taste, and feel our way around.

I have a protective shield behind my tiny head. It's called a **pronotum** (proh-no-tum). Not all insects have one of these.

Eyes—see p30 for more about our amazing eyes.

Six **legs** with joints in them (a joint is a bendy part, like your knee joint).

A hard outer case to protect the body. It's called an **exoskeleton**.

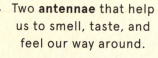

A body in three parts—a head, a thorax (the middle part), and an abdomen (the bottom part). My body parts are usually hidden but you can see them more clearly on an ant.

Most, though not all, insects have wings. I have one see-through soft pair of hindwings. They fold under a hard pair of wings that close up like a shell. The hard ones are called forewings or elytra (el-ee-tra).

My **elytra** open out when I need to fly.

My **hindwings** unfold when I need them.

When I'm flying my wings beat 85 times a second.

8

Many insects have wings that look different than beetle wings.

Lots of insects have different mouthparts to me because of the food they eat.

A leafcutter ant can slice off pieces of leaf.

A butterfly can suck up nectar.

True bugs are a particular group of insects that have a needle-like mouthpart to pierce plants or animals and suck up liquid. (They're the only ones that should really be called bugs, by the way, but we all get the nickname.)

Insects have been on Earth for roughly 400 million years. The largest insect that ever lived was a prehistoric creature, a bit like a dragonfly, with wings that stretched as wide as a crow's.

fossil

Half of all the known animal species on Earth are insects and there are probably lots more still to discover. There are way more insects than humans!

TEENY-TINY BUG FACT
We ladybugs can smell things with our feet! Lots of other insects can, too.

HOW THE BUTTERFLIES GOT THEIR COLOR

A bug tale from North America

A magic mixing bag captures summer's beauty

This magical tale is based on a legend of the Tohono O'odham Native American People who live in the Sonoran Desert in Arizona. It's about how butterflies came to be so colorful.

A kind spirit of goodness called Elder Brother watched over the Sonoran Desert People. One beautiful day he sat watching the children play, making sure they came to no harm. The sky was blue, the sunlight was sparkling on the green leaves of the trees, and the perfume of the red and yellow flowers was floating through the air.

However, as Elder Brother thought about the world, he began to feel sad.
"All this beauty will slip away when winter comes," he thought. "The leaves will fall. The flowers will die and the sky will turn from blue to gray. I really must do something to catch the beauty of the things I see today. I'll make something that will bring happiness to everyone."

He took out a magic bag and began to fill it. First he added a snippet of the blue sky. Then he popped in a red flower, a yellow flower, and a green leaf. He added lots of other colors, such as a silvery bird's feather. Finally, he sprinkled in some sunlight sparkles.

"Come and see what I've made," he called to the children. They gathered around as he shook and then opened the magic bag. A cloud of butterflies fluttered out, in every color imaginable. Their beauty made everyone feel glad and grateful for the world, just as Elder Brother wanted, and they still do. Remember that nature's beauty is a wonderful gift you can see every day.

I know that not all insects look beautiful to humans—but we're all interesting! Our bodies are just right for the lives we lead. Isn't nature incredible?

HOME SWEET HOME
Places we like to live

Insects make their homes in all sorts of different places across the world. You'll find us here, there, and pretty much everywhere!

Surviving in the city

Hiding from the heat

Insects live happily alongside humans even in big busy cities. For instance, around 17 billion ants are estimated to live in the city parks of New York City, USA! There's even a bee that digs out the mortar between building bricks to make a tiny nest hole. It's called a mortar bee or masonry bee.

In hot deserts insects usually burrow underground to hide in tunnels during the day. They will pop out at night when it's cooler, to hunt for food. Desert crickets and beetles all hide from the daytime sun.

A frozen habitat

A space home

Antarctica might be the coldest place on Earth, but it's still home to an insect. The Antarctic midge lives in pockets of soil around the edge of the frozen land. It spends most of its life as a little brown wormlike larva. Amazingly it can survive being frozen for up to 6 months.

In 1999 four ladybugs went to live in space onboard a NASA space shuttle. They took part in an experiment to see if they could catch aphids in weightless conditions. It turned out they could! They were nicknamed George, Paul, John, and Ringo after the world-famous Beatles pop group.

A TREE FOR ME

Trees make an ideal home for lots of insects. Here's why...

Trees make flowers in springtime. Inside each bloom there is sweet sugary nectar—food for insects such as bees and butterflies.

Leaves are foods for lots of insects such as caterpillars. Some birds eat insects, though, so there are also lots of birds living in trees!

Cracks and crevices in bark make good hiding places where insects can lay their eggs and shelter from the winter weather.

When a fallen tree branch starts to rot the wood gets soft and mushy. It's the perfect food for the larvae of some beetles (such as stag beetles and cockchafers). They hatch from eggs laid on the wood and will tunnel inside the log.

Thousands of mini insects live in soil and lay their eggs in the top layer. The eggs are small and white or pale yellow. They are sometimes laid in clusters (groups) of eggs.

Lots of insects live among the rotting leaves that fall from trees and carpet the ground in a forest. It's called leaf litter.

TEENY-TINY BUG FACT

Forty-three different types of ant were found living on just one rainforest tree in Peru, South America.

NIGHTTIME BUGS
Making use of moon and bug light

I go to sleep when it gets dark, but some insects wake up. Meet the moths and fireflies who fly around by the light of the Moon and stars.

Amazing moths

- Moths come out at night and are known as nocturnal creatures. They figure out which way to fly using the position of the Moon and the stars in the sky.

- Moths collect nectar from night-blooming flowers. They can find flowers in the dark because they can smell their scent, and can also detect a gas called carbon dioxide, given off by the blooms. Unlike humans, they can see a type of light called ultraviolet, which is reflected by the flower petals.

- There are roughly 160,000 different kinds of moths compared to just 17,500 types of butterflies.

- Some types of moths have a wingspan wider than this book! The biggest ones are found in tropical forests.

- The clearest difference between moths and butterflies is how they hold their wings when they are resting. Butterflies close up their wings like two hands together. Moths keep their wings spread. Moths also tend to be much fluffier than butterflies, which helps to keep them warm on chilly evenings.

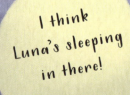

I think Luna's sleeping in there!

Luna's hiding place

Butterfly

Moth

Fantastic fireflies

★ Fireflies are a type of beetle. They are also called glow worms or lightning bugs.

★ The fireflies glow to attract each other, so they can pair up. Then the female will lay eggs. Each type of firefly has its own pattern of light flashes that you can see in the dark.

★ A male firefly makes its own light using chemicals in its body. It's a clever animal skill called bioluminescence (by-oh-loom-in-es-sents).

★ The light might be yellow, green, or orange. It's not hot like electric light would be, so it doesn't harm the firefly.

★ One species of female firefly is a deadly faker. They flash the signals of another species, luring the males in so that they can eat them!

At night insects are safe from hungry birds, but there is still danger from bats and owls who enjoy an insect snack.

TEENY-TINY BUG FACT
There are more than 2,000 different types of firefly, but some of them don't glow. Instead, they make special smells to attract each other.

BUG BUILDERS
The best tunnels, mounds, and towers

Ladybugs don't make nests but some insects I know are fantastic builders. They make homes to protect themselves and bring up their babies. I think it's time to give out my Bug Builders Awards!

 Best Team

Ants make a great building team. They work together to burrow out tunnels under the soil and make underground ant cities. Some ants also use twigs and leaves to make mounds above their tunnel cities. They live in the mounds in warm weather and hide underground when it's cold.

 Best Gluers

Weaver ants build their nests in tropical trees from southeast Asia down to Australia. Worker gangs of ants roll up leaves and then glue them in place using sticky silk made by their larvae. The ants usually create a nest about the size of a football.

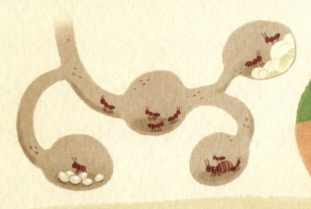

Weaver ants pulling a leaf together to glue it in place.

 The Champions

The award winners are the mound-building termites. They live in parts of Africa, South America, and Australia. The termites build a tall mud tower called a termitarium. It can reach up to 16.5 feet tall—taller than an adult African elephant.

The queen termite lays eggs inside the nest—one every three seconds. The workers hatch the babies in a nursery chamber.

Worker termites push pellets of chewed soil into the tower, where it dries hard. It takes them four or five years to finish building their hollow tower. After that they must keep repairing it.

Best Chewers

Wasps build nests by scraping up slivers of wood and chewing them to make a sticky pulp. The pulp dries to make a tough paper ball. Inside are six-sided (hexagonal) chambers to hold the wasp eggs. You might see a wasp nest in a sheltered spot such as under the roof of a building.

 Best Mini Builders

Caddis fly larvae live underwater in ponds and lakes until they are ready to hatch. To protect themselves from fish and bigger insects, they grab pieces of gravel, sand, twigs, and plants, and glue them into a case around their body. It looks like a tiny stony sleeping bag!

A wasp's nest only holds eggs and hatching wasps, not honey.

Bees are great builders, too. They make waterproof honeycomb using their body wax and use it to store honey as well as larvae. You can find out more about them later in this book.

Termites are farmers. They eat plants but can't digest the toughest stringiest bits. Instead they poop the chewed-up plant material into chambers inside their tower. They add fungus spores and it grows over the plant mush, turning it into crumbly compost that the termites can eat.

Enemies such as aardvarks and driver ants might attack a termitarium, but underneath there are underground escape tunnels for the termites to use.

TEENY-TINY BUG FACT
Up to two million termites might live inside a termitarium.

THE SONG OF THE CICADA

A bug tale from Ancient Greece
A bug becomes the star of the show

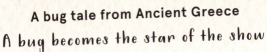

Cicadas live in warm countries, where they nestle in the grass. The loud chirruping sound of the males is hard to miss, so no wonder they have their own story!

Long, long ago in Ancient Greece there was a musician named Eunomos (you-no-mos). He played an instrument called a cithara (sith-ara), which had five strings like a guitar. Eunomos was a great cithara player and singer.

One day Eunomos heard about a music competition, which was to be held at the beautiful outdoor theater of Delphi. It would be a very grand occasion, as the theater could sit 5,000 people on its curved stone seats.

"To win, I'll need to practice a lot," he thought to himself, so he began practicing day and night until his family and neighbors complained. "Please stop! Your music is good but we're getting sick of it," they begged.

"OK. Sorry. I'll go and practice in the empty fields," agreed Eunomos and he took his instrument out to the countryside. The fields were home to the cicadas and they buzzed along as he played and sang.

On the day of the competition there were musicians playing pipes, harps, bells, and drums but Eunomos was confident he was the best. He proudly stood at the center of the stage and began plucking the cithara's strings. Up the notes he went, from the lowest to the highest, singing:

La, la, la, la...

PING!

The highest string broke! What a disaster. But a cicada from the fields had hidden itself in the folds of Eunomos' robe. It hopped out, sat on his cithara, and began to buzz the highest note. Between them they finished the song and—of course—won the competition!

SWIMMING BUGS
Hairy hunters and hatchers

Sit and watch a pond or a river on a warm sunny day and you'll see lots of busy insects. Let's see who's around...

Some insects can swim underwater. They have lots of tiny hairs on their body and a waxy body-coating, too. The wax keeps out water and the hairs trap air, so the insect gets surrounded by its own bubble of air to breathe as it dives underwater.

Insects such as water striders walk across the surface of the water. They have a clever secret—their very hairy legs! The tiny hairs trap air bubbles to help the insects float, rather like someone swimming held up by arm bands filled with air.

Water strider

As well as hungry fish lurking underwater, many pond insects are fearsome hunters themselves. For instance, whirligig beetles swim with their back legs, steer with their middle legs, and use their front legs to grab a victim.

Whirligig beetle

Giant water beetles will eat anything they can catch. Some types are nicknamed "toe biters" because they will even give a human swimmer a nip! The bite won't harm a human, but it is painful.

Giant water beetle

Water bugs such as the giant water beetle have a sharp beaklike mouthpart to pierce unlucky creatures. They inject poisonous spit that turns the prey into mush. Then they suck it up like a nightmare milkshake! Eek!

Lots of insects lay their eggs in freshwater. The eggs hatch into tiny wiggly larvae. They might live underwater for a while before they finally change into adults and fly above the water surface.

Water larvae often look like tiny underwater worms.

When warm weather comes, insects start to hatch. You might see a cloud of them above the water. They won't live for long, though. They will mate, lay eggs, and die. Then they might fall into the water and get gobbled up by fish.

Fly fishermen put a fake "fly" on a hook at the end of a fishing rod. The flies are feathery, with shiny beads, so they look like insects that have hatched from the water. The fishermen hope to fool fish into swimming up and eating the fly, so they get hooked.

TEENY-TINY BUG FACT
Ladybugs can paddle but we would drown underwater. We prefer land!

NOISY BUGS
Clever clicks and busy buzzing

Occasionally you might hear us insects. Apart from the buzzing of wings as we fly, some of us make noises to warn off attackers or to attract a mate.

Some insects rub body parts together to make a sound, often to show other insects how big and strong they are. It's called stridulation (strid-you-lay-shun). Grasshoppers rub their hind legs against their wings, while male crickets rub their wings together.

Male cicadas make a buzzing sound by flexing a body part called a tymbal. It's made of tiny ribs that pull and push together. African cicadas are the noisiest. Their sound can be almost as loud as a chainsaw!

CLICK, CLICK!

Some insects are good at mimicking—copying the sound of other insects. Australian katydids can mimic the noise of female cicadas to lure males near. Then... GULP! The male cicadas get eaten!

HISS!

Bats use high-pitched clicking sounds, called echolocation, to find tasty moths. The clicks bounce back from the moths so bats can sense where they are. However, some tiger moths and hawk moths make similar clicking sounds themselves to confuse the bats. Clever, huh?

TEENY-TINY BUG FACT
Ladybugs don't like loud noise. In tests, scientists found we didn't mind soft music but flew away when we heard loud rock!

When they feel threatened, cockroaches hiss by pushing air out through tiny tummy holes. Meanwhile deathwatch beetles create tunnels by gnawing wood and then bump their heads against the walls, making a "knock, knock" sound to attract a mate.

SQUEAK!

North American hawkmoth caterpillars can whistle! They make loud squeaks through their breathing holes, to scare away hungry birds.

BUZZ!

You can hear insects such as bees buzzing because their beating wings are moving air. Bees sometimes buzz louder inside flowers because they are vibrating, or moving, their bodies to shake pollen from the flower.

Many insects have their own version of ears, often in surprising places such as their knees or tummies. Most beetles don't have ears, though. We "hear" by sensing vibrations around us.

KNOCK, KNOCK!

HOW THE RACE WAS WON

A story from Brazil

A coat of many colors

Beetles might not get the insect award for air acrobatics, but we are often among the most colorful of the bugs. Here is a folk story from Brazil imagining how a rainbow-colored beetle came to be.

Long ago all jungle beetles were dull-colored. Not for them the flashy feathers of the jungle birds or the bright stripes and spots of the snakes and the butterflies. One day, a small brown beetle was slowly crawling along a fallen log on the jungle floor. She was inching forward, minding her own business, when a rat popped out.

"Look at you. You're so slow! You'll never get anywhere. Watch how it should be done," cried Rat. Then he began running along the top of the log and back again. "You could never beat me. I'm as speedy as can be!" he crowed.

A parrot had been listening and swooped down from the trees above.
 "Why don't you two have a race?" she suggested. "I'll get the jungle tailor bird to make the winner a bright new coat, in any color you want."
 "Yes, please. I'll have it gold and black like jaguar fur," cried Rat.
 "I sometimes dream of having a shiny rainbow coat," sighed the beetle.
 "Dream on, slowpoke," scoffed Rat.

The two animals lined up for the race and the parrot gave the starting signal.
 "Squawk! Go!"
At first Rat ran as fast as he could and left the beetle far behind. Then he began to slow down.
 "This is so easy I may as well just walk. There's no need to get out of breath," he thought to himself.

However, when Rat reached the finish line, he got a very big surprise indeed. The beetle was already there, as calm as you like.
 "Hey! How did you do that?" Rat spluttered. That's when the little beetle showed her secret by unfolding her hidden wings.
 "Nobody said we had to run, so I flew," she explained.
 "I didn't even know you had wings!" Rat gasped.
 "Never judge anyone by looks alone," chuckled the parrot. Then she arranged for the beetle to get her prize—a shimmering rainbow-colored coat that many jungle beetles still wear today.

GIANT FRIENDS
Who's the biggest?

It's time to meet some of the giants of the bug world. You'd have to go to tropical rainforests, hidden islands, or deserts to see them for yourself.

The **Royal Goliath beetle** is one of the world's beetle giants. The males can grow as long as an adult human hand. They live in steamy rainforest areas in southeast Africa.

The males have a Y-shaped horn on their heads, for fighting each other. They battle for food, a mate, and a place to live.

Goliath beetles usually eat sugary plant sap and fruit but they might munch on animal dung, too.

Male

2–4 inches long

Males are super-strong and they can lift about 850 times their own body weight. That's similar to you lifting a truck!

They have a pair of soft wings under a set of hard elytra—like mine but much bigger. When they fly, they make a loud thrumming noise.

Female

2–3 inches long

The females have shovel-shaped heads for digging into the soil, where they lay their eggs.

Goliath beetle larvae hatch under the soil. They can weigh up to 3.5 oz, which makes them twice as big as their parents!

There are around 3,000 different kinds of stick insects. The longest one also has a long name—**Phryganistria chinensis**. It's from China and it can grow up to 25 in long. That's roughly as long as an adult male human arm.

The world's biggest butterflies are found in tropical lands. The biggest one of all is the beautiful **Queen Alexandra's birdwing** from the Pacific island of Papua New Guinea.

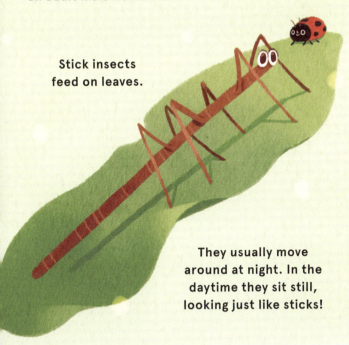

Stick insects feed on leaves.

They usually move around at night. In the daytime they sit still, looking just like sticks!

Birdwings feed on the nectar of flowers such as hibiscus blooms.

Females grow the biggest, with a wingspan up to 12 in (about as long as an ordinary ruler).

The **wētāpunga** is the world's heaviest insect. The females can grow to be heavier than a mouse and about as long as an adult human hand. To see them in the wild you'd have to travel to Little Barrier Island (Te Hauturu-o-Toi) off the coast of New Zealand.

Fossils show that they have been around for roughly 190 million years and lived on Earth at the same time as the dinosaurs.

Wētāpunga mainly feed on fresh leaves, usually at night.

A female might grow to about 4 in long.

TEENY-TINY BUG FACT
Most ladybugs are between 0.2 and 0.3 inch long, so we're not among the giants of the insect world!

THE TINIEST BUGS
Fairy-sized and feathery

You'd need a microscope to see the tiniest insects on the planet. We're big compared to them—but can you spot ten of us ladybugs in this flowerbed?

Fairy wasps live all over the world and most species are smaller than a pinhead. They have tiny feathery wings.

The smallest flying insect in the world is a fairy wasp called *kikiki huna*. Its name is Hawaiian and means *tiny bit*. It grows roughly 0.006 in long (about the same measurement as two human hairs side by side).

The tiniest flightless insect is a male fairy wasp that's only 0.005 in long. It's found in the US and it has a very long name—*Dicopomorpha echmepterygis*!

Fairy wasps aren't cute like storybook fairies, I'm afraid. They lay their eggs inside the eggs of other insects and the baby fairy wasps eat the contents.

Featherwing beetles are the smallest beetles of all. Most of them are less than 0.04 in long. Their wings are bristly fringes that move in an unusual figure-of-eight shape as they fly. They live among fallen leaves and logs, where they eat fungi.

The tiniest butterfly is the **pygmy blue**, found in North America. Its wingspan can be as small as ½ in, roughly the size of an adult human's little fingernail.

Mosquitos are small but nasty bloodsucking insects that can spread disease. The smallest one is the pale-footed uranotaenia from the southern USA. It measures 0.1 in long but doesn't drink human blood. It prefers to feed on frogs.

TEENY-TINY BUG FACT
The smallest ladybird species is 0.08–0.12 in long, roughly the size of two pinheads side by side.

WHAT WE SEE
Our brilliant bug eyes

Insects have eyes that look very different than human eyes. This means we see the world differently than you do.

Humans have two eyeballs, and each one contains a lens that brings you a picture of what you see. Your brain mixes the two pictures to make one. But insects have lots of lenses, sometimes thousands! Our eyes are called compound eyes.

Some of us have eyes on top of our heads and can see all the way around behind us (dragonflies, for example). That's good for spotting prey and for dodging enemies.

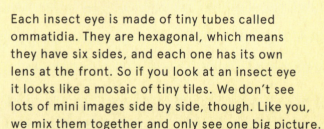

Ladybug eyes and antennae, close-up.

Some termites and insect larvae can see very little, and some have no eyes at all.

Each insect eye is made of tiny tubes called ommatidia. They are hexagonal, which means they have six sides, and each one has its own lens at the front. So if you look at an insect eye it looks like a mosaic of tiny tiles. We don't see lots of mini images side by side, though. Like you, we mix them together and only see one big picture.

Many insects can see ultraviolet light, a type of light invisible to humans. It gets reflected off objects such as flowers, helping insects to spot them.

Who sees what?

Insects have different numbers of ommatidia in their eyes. The ones with the most ommatidia see the most detail.

Butterflies and moths have around 17,000 ommatidia per eye. They are very short-sighted, but they can see a much wider picture than humans.

Some dragonflies have 30,000 or more ommatidia per eye. They're great at spotting movement, which is good for hunting. Some dragonflies have a darker part on top of their eyes. This may act like a pair of sunglasses to shield them from strong sunlight.

Honey bees have about 5,500 ommatidia per eye. They are really good at seeing purple, violet, and blue and they're much better than humans at seeing things when traveling fast.

Luna's eyesight test

What's my ladybug eyesight like? If I were to ever go to an insect optician, here's what the report would say. (It would be different for other insect species.)

- Luna can only see in black, white, and gray.
- Her eyesight is pretty blurry. She's very short-sighted and only really sees things close-up.
- She is attracted to light-colored flowers because they're the ones she sees best.
- She can't see in the dark at all.

TEENY-TINY BUG FACT

Caterpillars can barely see at all and rely on sensing or feeling things around them instead.

MOST AMAZING
Incredible insect superpowers

If you are surprised by how we see, get ready to be truly amazed by some of the other talents we have!

TEENY-TINY BUG FACT
Ladybugs sometimes fly up to 3,668 feet high—higher than hot air balloons. We also hitch rides on planes, cars, boats, and trains!

THE BEST AIR ACROBAT
Dragonflies have bodies and wings shaped rather like airplanes, and like an acrobatic plane they can do some stunning tricks. They catch flies with their feet in midair and can eat hundreds of mosquitos a day.

Zoom

THE HIGHEST FLYER
Bumblebees have been spotted on mountainsides at heights of 18,0000 feet. Tests suggest they could fly even higher.

Buzz...buzz

THE BEST JUMPER
The **Little Froghopper** holds the record with a 27.5 in jump, though it's only ¼ in long. That's a bit like a man jumping over a 72-story skyscraper in one leap. Froghoppers usually live in among wild plants in Europe, North America, and Africa.

Ready... steady...

THE BEST SURVIVOR IN HOT WEATHER
The **Saharan silver ant** can go out in heat that would instantly shrivel other insects in its African desert home. It waits until all its enemies (such as hungry lizards) have hidden from the searing midday sunshine. Then it runs over burning sand on its long legs.

Sizzle...sizzle...

...spin!

...loop the loop

THEIR SECRET

A dragonfly can fly backwards, spin in mid-air, fly upside down or hover like a helicopter. That's because its wings can move separately to each other—up and down or backwards and forward. It can adjust them to move in lots of different ways.

...fly up high!

THEIR SECRET

Bumblebees are good at flying and sometimes even nesting in cold high locations because they have such thick fuzzy coats. Their hair is longer than other bees.

boing!

THEIR SECRET

The froghopper's legs have very strong muscles. They contract, or squeeze, and lock in place, a bit like a string pulled back on a bow and arrow. Then...boing, the froghopper takes off in a millisecond.

run, little ant!

THEIR SECRET

The top and sides of this ant's body are covered in tiny silvery hairs which reflect hot sunlight away, so it's just like it's wearing a coat of mirrors!

WHY THE ANTS CAN NEVER WIN

A story from South Africa
A wise king shows the way

Life in the wild is tough: big animals eat little animals and that's what this story is about. It's based on a folk tale from South Africa.

The ants were fed up with having so many enemies. Aardvark liked to slurp them up with his long tongue and Lizard grabbed them for a snack whenever he could. Then there were all the hungry birds. The danger was never-ending, and the ants wanted to make it stop.

The different species of ants held a meeting to find the answer.
 "We should build safe dens underground," some cried.
 "No! Let's build nests above ground," shouted another group.
 "That won't do. We need to live up in the trees," another group insisted.

The ants couldn't agree so they all went back to their homes and did what they thought best. Some of the ants built a den underground.
 "This is safe from big old Aardvark and those greedy birds," they said, but it turned out that Lizard could wriggle in and reach a few of them with his flicking tongue.

Some of the ants built a den above ground.
  "This is too strong for Lizard or the pesky birds," they agreed, but it turned out that Aardvark could break in with his sharp claws and lick up an ant meal or two.

Some of the ants climbed up to live in tree holes. They were safe from Aardvark up there, but Lizard could climb along the branches and it was perfect for the birds.

"We failed! We should have found a way to work together," the ants cried, and began to blame each other. Eventually the wise King of the Insects (the biggest beetle in the land) called the ant leaders to his palace hidden under the bushes.
  "Working together is a good thing," he explained, "but every creature in the world can't do that. It's impossible. My advice for everyone—bugs big and small—is this: do your best with the world you have."

The Insect King was right. You can't stop wild creatures from eating each other because they're all connected. Some eat plants. Others eat the plant-eaters and each other. The connections are called a food chain or a food web.

THE GRUESOME GANG
Grabbers, sprayers and chasers...Eek!

Some of us insects are fearsome hunters with special tricks and weaponry as deadly as any cartoon supervillain. Meet an especially gruesome gang. Luckily they are all way smaller than humans!

🌸 PRAYING MANTIS

Home: Worldwide

Weaponry: Forelegs armed with hooks and spikes, for grabbing food.

Prey: Insects and lizards.

Top hunting skill: Speed. It sits completely still, waiting for prey to come near. Then it ambushes them incredibly quickly.

🌸 CREMATOGASTER ANT

Home: Africa

Weaponry: A spray of toxic venom that paralyzes its victims.

Top hunting skill: It raises up its sting like a hosepipe, and shoots poison into the air. It can aim the sting in any direction.

Prey: Termites, mainly.

🌸 ASSASSIN BUG

Home: Worldwide

Prey: Bees, wasps, dragonflies, beetles, and other flies.

Weaponry: Deadly spit that kills instantly and turns the insides of the prey to liquid.

Top hunting skill: Perches somewhere and waits for a victim to fly by. Then it gives chase, bites its prey, and injects poisonous spit.

ANTLION LARVAE

Home: Worldwide

Weaponry: Big cutting jaws, pincers, and venom.

Top hunting skill: Digs a funnel-shaped pit hidden among leaf litter, for passing ants to fall into.

Prey: Mostly juicy ants.

ARMY ANT

Home: Tropical parts of the world

Weaponry: A sting plus sharp jaws like a pair of scissors.

Top hunting skill: Working together. A swarm of thousands might mount a raid, streaming out of their nest in columns to grab whatever they can find.

Prey: Any small animals in their path.

TIGER BEETLE

Home: Different species worldwide

Prey: Aphids, caterpillars, all sorts of small insects, and even slugs. It eats its own body weight in food every day.

Top hunting skill: Running across the ground on its long legs. It's one of the fastest bug runners.

Weaponry: Swordlike harp jaws.

TEENY-TINY BUG FACT
Insects that hunt actually help humans by eating pests such as mosquitos and greenfly.

FIGHT BACK!
How to beat the gruesome gang

Though we might have enemies bigger and fiercer than us, we insects sometimes have surprising defences of our own. It's time to let you know some top-secret skills!

ACID

If it's threatened, the **red wood ant** can spray out acid that's powerful enough to eat through its enemy's skin.

PINCERS AND POISON PAINT

Soldier **termites** have long pincers to defend their nest from invaders. Some even have an extra-long nose which they use like a paintbrush to smear poison on their enemies.

SUPER-HOT POISON

When **bombardier beetles** are threatened, they fire out an explosive stream of poisonous chemicals, as hot as boiling water. Toads like eating beetles but they'll quickly spit one of these yucky bombardiers out!

PATTERNS TO FOOL YOU

Butterflies and moths sometimes have eye spots on their outstretched wings, thought to help scare off predators. It's possible they might startle an enemy into thinking the butterfly or moth is a bigger creature, perhaps a bird or even an owl.

DON'T MESS WITH LADYBIRDS!

Red, yellow, and black are a kind of danger sign for creatures. They send a message—THIS CRITTER MIGHT BE POISONOUS. Our bright ladybug colors are a warning to animals that we might taste bad, and we do!

I remember these spotted red bugs taste yucky.

Our colors and spot patterns make us easier for birds to remember. They won't forget that we taste bad!

We squeeze out a stinky chemical mixture called pyrazine through our leg joints if we are threatened.

We also defend ourselves by "playing dead"—drawing our legs in and sitting absolutely still.

Harlequin ladybugs are a problem for other types of ladybugs (though not for humans). They are spreading around the world and they have an extra-big appetite. Not only do they take all the aphid food, they also eat our eggs and larvae. They have similar colors and spots as the rest of us, but they have orange tummies and legs, while most of us have black tummies and legs.

TEENY-TINY BUG FACT
Ladybugs might bite if threatened, though we can't nip through human skin.

ACTING STARS
The art of clever camouflage

Some bugs are masters of disguise, as good at acting as any film star. They might use their disguise to hunt, or to hide from enemies.

The North American lunar moth looks exactly like a leaf when it sits still with its green wings open.

A thorn bug has a curved spiky back, so when it sits on a plant stem, it looks just like a thorn. It lives in the Americas and parts of Asia.

No wonder the dead leaf mantis lurks among fallen leaves in its Malaysian home. Its prey won't spot this hungry enemy until it's too late!

The flat bark bug looks just like a knobbly section of tree bark, the perfect woodland disguise. It's found in most parts of the world.

BRAVO!

SUPERB!

A sand grasshopper is colored just like grains of sand. It's really hard to spot on the North American prairies, where it hides out in sandy locations.

The orchid mantis pretends to be a pretty bloom full of yummy pollen and nectar for visiting insects in South Asian forests. In fact, those insects end up being the meal!

We've heard about stick insects already (see page 27) but their southeast Asian cousins the walking leaf insects are pretty amazing, too. They have a long body that looks like a branch of leaves. They grow about as long as the palm of an adult human hand.

Peppered moths are speckled, as if they've been showered with pepper from a pepper shaker. It makes them super-hard to see against pale-colored tree trunks covered in lichen. They live in Europe and North America.

WONDERFUL WORK!

TEENY-TINY BUG FACT
The orchid mantis can change color to blend in with its background.

THE WORLD NEEDS BUGS!
An insect SOS

Insects are vital to our planet because we help plants grow and we eat up lots of the pests that harm humans and crops. Some of us are even helpful planet cleaners—munching up waste such as dead leaves and even dead creatures. But we're in real trouble. Our numbers are falling, and we need your help.

Humans need to find ways to reduce harmful pollution, such as that caused by burning coal or oil. Using power from the sun and wind is much kinder to the planet.

Wind turbines turn wind into power.

Solar panels turn sunlight into power.

CAFE

WE USE ORGANIC INGREDIENTS

Organic means no harmful chemicals were used to help grow the ingredients.

Vegetable garden

Harmful chemicals used in farming are a big reason bugs are dying out. You humans can help by pushing for farms to use fewer and safer chemicals. Also, if you have room, try growing your own vegetables without using chemicals.

A wildflower meadow gives us lots of food.

Ninety percent of flowering plants rely on insects visiting them to feed on nectar. Pollen is dusted onto the insect when it visits and gets brushed off when it lands on a different flower.

The pollen then joins with egg cells inside the flower to make seeds. It's called pollination, and the more pollinating insects—such as bees and moths—there are around, the better.

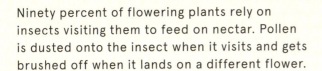

Parks and green spaces in towns and cities are good for us as they tend to have lots of flowers and ponds, too. Cutting the grass a lot and using weedkiller destroys the wildflowers many of us rely on, so it needs to be avoided.

A pond makes a great home for insects if it's looked after and kept clean.

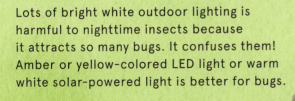

Lots of bright white outdoor lighting is harmful to nighttime insects because it attracts so many bugs. It confuses them! Amber or yellow-colored LED light or warm white solar-powered light is better for bugs.

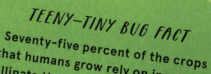

TEENY-TINY BUG FACT
Seventy-five percent of the crops that humans grow rely on insects to pollinate them. You definitely need us!

BE A LADYBUG FRIEND
Make a cosy flowery home

There are lots of things you can do to help all the friendly little bugs who live near you. In return some of us will eat up the pesky aphids who attack your plants, while some of us will pollinate your flowers for you.

MAKE A LADYBIRD LODGE

Build a lodge to help ladybugs sleep through the winter in a safe place. Position it in a sheltered spot that won't get too hot or cold, for example against a wall or a shed.

You will need:

- Some dry pine cones
- Dry twigs and leaves
- Any hollow twigs you find
- Two spare roof tiles or two scrap pieces of wood to make the roof

Pile the pine cones, twigs, and sticks on the ground. Then lay the tiles or pieces of scrap wood over them like a house roof, to keep them dry. Fill in any gaps with more dry leaves.

If you don't have tiles or wood for the roof you could stuff your cones and sticks into an old flowerpot or two, and lay them sideways. Use stones to wedge them in a safe spot.

PLANT FOR US

Even if you don't have a garden, ladybugs might visit if you grow plants in pots on your windowsill or doorstep. Here are some flowering plants that attract ladybugs looking for aphids.

HELP US STAY OUTDOORS

Ladybugs sometimes come indoors for our winter sleep, but it's not good for us. If the heating comes on, we could wake up at the wrong time, when there are no aphids to eat. If you find a ladybug indoors in the winter, gently take it outside and put it in a hidden sheltered place, safe from harm.

Too many aphids will damage a plant
but we can help by munching them up!
We'll spread smiles when we visit you
and fill our tiny tummies, too.

And when you see a ladybug
stretching out its little wings,
ready to take off and go...
tell them Luna says hello!

Luna the ladybug

Welcome to my honey hive home.
It's where I live with my family.
I'm small and fuzzy and striped black and gold.
I'm Buzzwing the hard-working honey bee!

Dear Reader,

Bees like me live around the world, in jungles and cities as well as in meadows like mine. What are we doing, so busy and buzzy? I will show you. Come with me. You can visit my home and join me on my travels.

Honey bees have been making honey since the first people walked the Earth and the first stories were told. I'll tell you some tales from long ago of magical bees and wondrous honey as gold as sunshine in a pot.

As we fly through the book you can play my finding game. There are hidden things and friends to spot. I'll start you off on this page. Can you find my neighbor, Whisker Mouse?

Buzzwing the honey bee

WHEN BUZZWING WAS BORN
Bee friends and busy work

One sunny day, inside our hive,
my mother, the Queen, laid an egg.
It was me...
but I was not yet a bee!

After three days I hatched as a wiggly
grub, munching up honey and pollen.
I grew and grew,
and grew and grew...
Then turned into something new
inside a soft cocoon,
and then...

I popped out as a worker bee.
That's me!

As soon as I was born I met the other bees who live in my hive.

The worker bees (like me)
We run the hive and make
the honey. There are
thousands of us.

The Queen bee
She is the bee mother,
who lays the eggs. There
is only one of her.

The drones
They are the bee dads.
There are just a few
hundred of them.

We worker bees run the hive,
so I got to work straight away,
changing my jobs as I grew older.

First I was a cleaner,
tidying the hive.

Then I was a nurse,
looking after the babies.

Then I made the honey and wax.

Then I was a guard at the door.

At last, I flew outside,
collecting sweet nectar
and yellow pollen.
I am Buzzwing,
the bringer of goodness!

Can you spot Lacey Ladybird and her two sisters
in the meadow near my hive?

ALL ABOUT BEES
Hairy eyes and a honey tummy

I'm an insect. I have three body parts. A head, a thorax (my middle section) and an abdomen (my tail end). I have six legs too.

Antennae

Head and eyes

Forewings

Thorax

Hindwings

Abdomen

Pollen sac

Sting

I have two sets of **buzzy wings** that I can beat up to 230 times a second. They make the air vibrate (shake), which makes a buzzing sound.

I am 13–17 millimetres (about ½ inch) long, roughly the size of a grown-up's fingernail.

I am **hairy and stripy.** My thorax is hairy and my abdomen is striped yellow and black.

Each of my **back legs has a pollen sac**, like a tiny bag, for carrying the pollen I collect.

I use my **two antennae** to touch, taste, smell, and detect movement. This is useful because a hive is very dark. I can smell about 40 times better than you humans.

My tail end has a **sting**, in case I get attacked. It's sharp so it can puncture skin like a needle!

I have three simple eyes called ocelli, and **two amazing eyes**, called compound eyes. Each is made of 6,900 tiny lenses that fit together like a mosaic.

Guess what! **My eyeballs are hairy**! The tiny hairs probably sense air moving, helping me to fly on windy days.

I use my long tongue, called my proboscis, to suck up nectar. It goes into my **honey stomach**, which is separate from my ordinary stomach. Find out more on page 66.

THE BABY AND THE BEES

A bee tale from Greece

A magical springtime journey

This story of how we honey bees got our color goes back thousands of years to the time of the Ancient Greeks. They had lots of legends about magical gods, and the most powerful one of all became a friend of the bees.

In the lands of Ancient Greece there was once a mighty King of the Gods called Cronus, who was a monstrous giant. Even his own family were not safe from his greed and madness.

When Cronus's wife gave birth to a baby boy, called Zeus, she knew he was in great danger. She crept secretly away and journeyed to the beautiful island of Crete, hidden in the sparkling blue sea, far away from the cruel King. There she found a cave high in the mountains, where she hid her precious son.

Baby Zeus was cared for by two magical spirits of Crete – Almathea the goat and Melissa the nymph. Almathea fed the baby cool creamy goat's milk. Melissa gave him delicious honey made by the bees who lived in the cave. Every day they flew around the island collecting the sweetest nectar from wild flowers to make into a treat for their precious little baby. These bees were strange-looking, and grey like the walls of their cave.

Zeus grew strong and powerful, and eventually he left Crete to defeat Cronus and become the King of the Gods. He never forgot the sweetness of his childhood honey, though. He rewarded the honey bees by turning them a beautiful golden and black – golden like the sunsets of Crete, and black like the wood of a warming Cretan fire.

The legendary story of Zeus and the bees is like a beautiful dream, isn't it? The real reason we honey bees have our golden and black colors is probably because they scare off animals who would like to eat us. They are a sort of danger sign to show that we are poisonous. Clever, eh?

Can you spot a small lizard somewhere on the island?

A HAPPY HIVE HOME
In and out, safe and sound

Wild honey bees live in nests they build themselves, in hidden places such as tree holes. I live in a hive given to us by the beekeeper. It looks like a little wooden block of apartments. I fly in and out on my collecting trips, making as many as 12 trips a day if the weather is good. I visit up to 100 flowers each time I go out.

I am a fantastic navigator. I can remember the area around my home and I navigate by checking the position of the sun in the sky. Considering my brain is the size of a sesame seed, I'm pretty smart, don't you think?

I don't leave my hive on very cold days. On very hot days we collect water in our mouths and spit it into our hive. We then fan our wings to cool the hive.

A place where there are lots of beehives together is called an apiary.

Can you spot Coco, the beekeeper's cat?

The beekeeper puts rows of wooden frames inside the hive for us. We build our honeycombs inside the frames.

Our hive has different sections, like floors in a block of apartments. This helps our beekeeper to look after us. She can check on separate parts of the hive, one by one. Find out more about her visits on page 82.

In years gone by, humans made beehives from woven baskets called skeps. Even thousands of years ago in the time of Ancient Egypt, there were beehive baskets.

We bees have made delicious honey for Pharaohs, Emperors, Chieftains, Kings, and Queens...

... for everyone, big and small, rich or poor. Hooray for honey hives everywhere!

COME INSIDE
Bee food and bee babies

Inside the hive there are thousands of bees crawling this way and that, like people in a busy city. We are all working together to look after our babies, make food, and keep our home clean and tidy.

Worker bee

Some worker bees build honeycomb. They use beeswax, which they make inside their bodies, to form the hexagonal honeycomb holes, called cells. Other bees are kept busy cleaning the hive and throwing out any trash.

Queen **Eggs**

The Queen bee lays eggs in some of the honeycomb cells. At first, the eggs look like tiny white seeds. They then become little white grubs. Worker bees feed the grubs with a mixture of honey and pollen called "bee bread." Eventually they hatch into adult bees, ready to join in the work of the hive.

Grub being fed

Bee hatching

If the hive needs a new Queen, some of the grubs are fed a special food called "Royal Jelly," which helps them grow into Queens.

Some of the honeycomb cells are used for storing pollen or honey that has been made by the worker bees. Honey that is ripe and ready to eat is covered over with a lid of wax, like the lid on a jar.

Pollen

Honey

The honey in here is ready to eat

Some worker bees guard the hive and will chase away any bee that does not belong. They can tell by the way a bee smells. We all smell the same in our hive—the same smell our Queen has. Can you see worker bees gathering around her to look after her?

Can you see a drone? He is bigger than the worker bees and he doesn't have a sting.

THE LADY OF THE MOON

A tree tale from Australia

A honey treat and a sweet good turn

The beekeeper likes to talk to us when she comes to visit. She told us this tale early one morning, when dew covered the meadow like tiny glass beads scattered across the grass. The legend comes from Australia, where it has been told for centuries by the wonderful storytellers of the Aborigine people. It's the legend of the Moon Lady.

The beautiful Moon Lady lived way up high above the clouds. She drifted across the sky day and night, looking down on the bush country below. The Aborigine people knew she was there and that she sometimes came down to visit when nobody was around. They would leave her treats to find, such as pieces of delicious, golden honeycomb.

One day she watched from above as the human honey hunters went about their work. They found a wild bee nest high in a tree and gathered honey and honeycomb to take home. They didn't forget to leave her something, though. She watched as they placed a chunk of honeycomb in a hollow log, ready for her visit.

When it was quiet she drifted down and was surprised to see how dry the countryside was.
 "It's a shame there has been no rain here for a while," she thought to herself.

She put her arm in the hollow log to collect the honeycomb, but when she tried to pull it out again, she found that her arm and the honeycomb were stuck!

However hard she pulled and wriggled her arm, she could not free herself.
 "Whatever shall I do? I must return to the sky or there will be no moonlight ever again," she cried.

Then she heard light footsteps behind her. The humans had seen her and they had come to help. They gently freed her arm so that she could return to the sky.

"One good turn deserves another," she smiled before she left. "I can see how dry your land is, so I will send refreshing dew every morning for you and all the plants and animals to drink."

We should all think of the Moon Lady when we see the morning dew, and remember that it is good to do kind things. Like honey, they are sweet!

BRILLIANT BEE DANCE
Watch me waggle

After a trip, I go back to my hive and tell the other bees where I have found plants full of nectar or pollen. I don't talk, so how can I let them know where to go? I do something amazing. I dance out a message!

I walk along the honeycomb in a straight line, waggling my body, and I also go around in a figure 8. The straight line part of my dance is called my waggle run.

Waggle run

Think of the position of the sun as 12 o'clock on a clock face. If my waggle run goes straight forward then the other bees know that the flowers are in the direction of the sun.

If I do my waggle run at an angle, then the other bees can tell exactly what direction I am signaling compared to the sun. Think of the other numbers on a clock face, going around from the 12. I'm signaling toward one of those. The angle of the waggle run below is like 2 o'clock on a clock face.

I send messages about distance too. The longer my waggle run is, the farther away the flowers are.

If I shake my body a lot it means: "There's lots to collect in the flower patch I found. We need lots of bees to go now!"

If I walk around the hive shaking my legs it means: "I need some help here! I've brought in a lot of nectar and I need more bees to help process it."

No other animal dances a message like we do. We're the dance champions!

FLY THE MEADOW
Invisible patterns and tasty food

In springtime, we worker bees are kept busy flying between the flowers in the meadow.

I visit one kind of flower on each trip I make. Some flower pollen sticks to my hairy body and I carry it to the next flower.

A flower can only make seeds if it gets pollen from another similar flower. I do the job of carrying the pollen, which is called pollination.

I will take some pollen home to feed the other bees, along with sweet nectar from inside the flowers. We make that into honey.

My thousands of tiny eye lenses help to make my sight super-powered. I can see in great detail.

Can you spot a butterfly perched among the meadow flowers? She is feeding on nectar too.

FLY AWAY, BEES
A new Queen and a new home

In late springtime, a hive sometimes gets too full of bees. Then some of the worker bees and drones will fly away with their Queen to find a new home.

Before the Queen leaves, the workers will raise a new Queen. They will build special extra-big cells called Queen cells. The old Queen will lay eggs in the cells, and the workers will feed them on "Royal Jelly" when they hatch, to turn them into Queens. There is only room for one Queen in a hive. When the first one hatches, she will kill the other grubs, so that only she will reign.

The old Queen will leave the hive with about half of the workers and some of the drones. This is called swarming. If you see a swarm, don't be scared. The bees are busy following their Queen and they're not likely to bother you.

At first the swarm will settle somewhere near their old hive, in a big ball of bees that buzzes loudly.

All the bees in the hive obey the Queen, and know just what to do to help her. That's because she sends out chemical signals called pheromones—a kind of bee perfume full of messages.

Can you spot a hungry blackbird looking for a worm?

Bzzz

The swarm will send out bee scouts to find a new home.

Then the whole swarm will move on.

If you see bees swarming, tell a grown-up. They can phone a local beekeeper to come and collect the swarm and give it a safe new home, as it is hard for honey bees to survive in the wild. Find out more on page 82.

SUMMER SWEET
Busy, busy making honey

In summer we gather lots of nectar and make plenty of delicious honey. There will be enough to feed us and some for you too!

How do bees make honey?

1. When a worker bee comes back to the hive she pushes nectar up into her mouth from her honey stomach.

2. The nectar is transferred into the mouths of other worker bees, to get rid of the water in the nectar. It does no harm and we bees add useful chemicals called enzymes, which kill off bacteria.

3. When the nectar is thick enough we store it in a honey cell.

Which honey do you like?

Honey tastes and looks different depending on the kind of nectar we harvest. Buy some honey from a local beekeeper and ask them which plants they think made it.

Honey can be runny or thick, depending on how much water it has in it. Do you like thick honey or runny honey?

How much honey?

A bee carries a tiny amount of nectar back from each trip.

It takes around 22,700 flying trips to make enough honey to fill one ordinary-sized 16 ounce (450 g) jar. On those trips, we bees would need to visit about 2 million flowers and fly around 54,600 miles (88,000 km) between us.

We make around 1,760 pounds (800 kg) of honey in the hive in a year. We will eat lots of it but there will be plenty stored too.

A worker bee will make about $1/12$ of a teaspoon of honey in a lifetime. That's why we need so many busy bees in our hive!

Why is honey good for you?

A small spoonful of honey will help soothe your sore throat if you have a cough. It's similar to taking cough medicine.

Honey is sometimes used to help heal wounds because it is good at killing off bacteria. That's because of the enzymes we bees add to it.

THE BOY WHO ATE SKY HONEY

A bee tale from India

A golden sky and a poem to write

Have you ever heard someone compare words to honey? They might say: "Those are honeyed words," meaning they sound beautiful. This story is about a lucky young man called Kahsivat, who found honeyed words long ago in Ancient India.

Kahsivat was an ordinary young man. He was good at some things—helping to look after his family's goats, for instance—and he was not bad at singing to them to keep them happy in the field. But nobody would call him extraordinary… until one morning when his luck changed.

Kahsivat was out early with the goats, just after dawn. He loved this time of day because, as the sun rose, the sky looked as if it was painted gold like the ceiling of a palace. Kahsivat did not know it, but far above his head in the realm of the Hindu gods, Ushas the goddess of the dawn was turning the sky gold as she rode across it in a chariot pulled by winged horses.

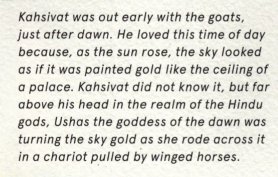

She was followed by her twin brothers, two gods called the Ashvins. They also rode in a chariot and they always carried some pots of their favourite food – delicious magical honey – on their journey.

As Kahsivat looked up and admired the beautiful sky, some drops of honey fell from one of the pots down toward the goat herd. Perhaps he caught them on his fingers and licked them, or perhaps they dropped straight into his mouth as he yawned in the early sunlight. Nobody knows, but when Kahsivat next began to sing to his goats, his words were the sweetest poetry.

When Kahsivat went back to his village, his family and friends were astounded by his wonderful songs and poems. His fame soon spread far and wide and he went on to become a great Indian poet, famed for his magical honeyed words!

Perhaps you could write some poetry like Kahsivat. Here are some words about honey and bees that you could put in your poem.

- Golden
- Shiny
- Sweet
- Treat
- Busy
- Buzzy
- Furry
- Flying

Can you spot a little monkey somewhere on this page?

BUZZING AROUND THE WORLD
Big, tiny, furry, shiny... BEES!

There are lots of different types of bees living around the world. We are different colors and sizes. We might be as big as your thumb or as tiny as grains. We might be as furry as a teddy bear or even green as grass!

There are about 20,000 different types of bees in the world, and only a few make honey. The bees in my hive are called *Western honey bees*.

The biggest bee in the world is the Wallace's giant bee. It grows as big as an adult's thumb, and it buzzes very loudly! It lives on an Indonesian island and makes its nest from tree resin, instead of wax.

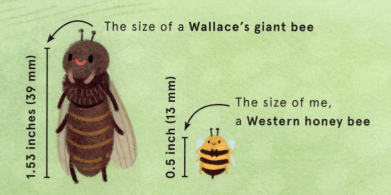

The size of a **Wallace's giant bee**
1.53 inches (39 mm)

The size of me, a **Western honey bee**
0.5 inch (13 mm)

Wallace's giant bees are very rare. Nobody saw one for many years and people thought they had died out forever, until one was spotted in 2019. Good luck, giant bees. I hope there are many more of you hidden on your island!

Bees can be black, orange, white, red, green, blue, or even purple! Different sorts of orchid bees are especially brightly colored, and often shiny too, like little flying jewels. They live in the Americas.

The size of an **Orchid bee**
Up to 1.2 inches (30 mm)

My friends the wild bumblebees are much hairier than me. Find out more about them on page 76.

0.07 inch (1.8 mm)
The size of a **Quasihesma bee**

Australian male Quasihesma bees and American Perdita bees are just a tiny bit bigger than two sugar grains. They are the tiniest bees in the world.

Some bees are very furry. There's a bee in Australia called the Teddy Bear bee because of its thick orange-brown hairs. Look out for bees with extra-hairy legs too.

0.6 inch (15 mm)
The size of a **Teddy Bear bee**

The Himalayan giant honey bee is the largest honey-making bee in the world. It lives in nests high up on mountainsides in the Himalayas. Local people say the nests are guarded by magical mountain spirits.

The size of a **Himalayan giant honey bee**
1.2 inches (30 mm)

HONEY THIEVES
Stay away, sneaky stealers!

Some wild animals are my enemies. They like to steal honey and even eat bees! The biggest thieves are those lumbering, furry greedyguts – the bears.

No hive or bee nest is safe in places where wild bears live. Bears can smell honey from far away.

They will do anything to get to the honey treat, and will even climb a tall tree to get to a wild bee nest.

Bears will put up with stings to get to the honeycomb – the treat they like the best.

One honey farmer in Turkey decided to use his local honey-stealing bears to help him test honey. He put out bowls filled with different kinds of honey and filmed the bear thieves in the night to see which honey they liked the best. Those furry guzzlers liked the most expensive one!

★ WANTED ★

Here are some other beastly enemies we bees never want to come across.

Honey badger

The honey badger lives in Africa and Asia. It uses its claws to rip open nests and hives.

Hive beetle

Mini enemies such as hive beetles and mites can make a whole hive of bees get sick and die.

Bee-eater

Some birds like to gobble up bees. There's even a type of bird called a bee-eater.

Kinkajou

Kinkajous are also called honey bears. They are not really bears, but they are definitely honey thieves in the South American jungles where they live.

CHEE-CHEE, COME WITH ME
A honey-taking team

One summer's day I heard some birds – the swifts – calling to each other as they flew across the meadow. They were telling tales of their winter spent in Africa. I heard with amazement about a southern African bird that guides humans to wild bee nests.

The bird is called the **greater honeyguide**. The honey-hunting humans know how to call it down from the trees.

"Brrrr... hm, brrrrrr... hm," call the humans.

"Chee, chee," replies the bird.

The little brown bird guides the hunters to a bee nest. It might be high up in a tree, so the hunters must climb the trunk.

The hunters blow smoke into the nest to calm the bees. Our beekeeper does that sometimes too (see page 83).

The humans break open the nest to take the honey, and the greater honeyguide gets its reward. It eats the bee grubs and the wax too.

I don't like the sound of this bird because I am a honey bee, but I have to admit that it is very clever. The way these birds work together with humans is very rare in the animal world.

Can you see a little snake hiding somewhere in the African forest?

HIDEY-HOLE HOMES
Burrows, shells and stony nests

My friends the bumblebees don't live in a hive. Come and see where they have made their home, in the field where the lambs play. You can also find out about some bees that make tiny nests all on their own.

Bumblebees nest in holes, such as abandoned animal burrows or hollow logs. There might be 50-100 of them in one nest, which is much messier and more untidy than a honey bee home like mine.

Look for different types of bees popping in and out of their nest entrances.

Solitary bees live on their own and they don't make honey or wax. There are lots of different kinds, such as mason bees, mining bees and carpenter bees.

The mason bee puts some pollen and nectar inside a hole, then lays an egg and builds a tiny wall of mud in front of it to keep it safe.

Mason bees live in many parts of the world. The females nest in holes or cracks they find in stones. One type of mason bee even likes to nest inside empty snail shells.

Mining bees also live in many places across the world. They dig tunnels in the soil and lay an egg underground, along with some pollen for the larvae to eat when they hatch.

Carpenter bees usually live in warm parts of the world. They gnaw tunnels in wood and lay their eggs inside.

You might see a mining bee going in and out of a hole with a small mound of soil around it. 70 per cent of the world's bee species live underground.

Most solitary bees are small and harmless, and they are very good for flowers. Don't worry if you see them buzzing around where you live.

Can you spot a caterpillar in the lambs' meadow?

HOW THE ELEPHANTS GOT THEIR TRUNKS

A bee tale from Thailand

Some fiery friends who wouldn't leave

I heard this funny story from a bee, who heard it from another bee and another bee... in a buzzy storytelling line that reaches across the world. It's an old, old tale from Thailand about bees nesting in the wrong place.

In ancient times, when the world was young, the elephants in Thailand did not have long trunks and the wild bees did not build their nests inside hollow trees. Instead, the elephants had short snouts and the bees nested on branches in the open air.

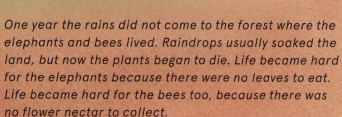

One year the rains did not come to the forest where the elephants and bees lived. Raindrops usually soaked the land, but now the plants began to die. Life became hard for the elephants because there were no leaves to eat. Life became hard for the bees too, because there was no flower nectar to collect.

The sun beat down and soon a spark crackled and kindled among the dry wood of the forest floor. A tree caught fire. Then another and another... until a curtain of flames began to sweep across the whole forest!

The elephants tried to run to safety but they didn't know which way to go. They soon grew tired, but could hear the roar of the flames not far behind.

"Help, somebody. Help!" they cried.

"We'll show you the way out if you give us a lift to safety," buzzed the bees.

"Of course," agreed the elephants and they opened their mouths.

The bees flew inside and settled in the cool darkness of the elephants' snouts. From there they guided the elephants to a lake where they could wade into the water and stay safe until the forest fire burnt out.

But...

... when it was time for the elephants to return to the land, the bees refused to leave their cosy new homes. The elephants trumpeted and blew and trumpeted and blew for hours and hours to get rid of the bees. They did it for so long that their trunks stretched to the size they are today.

In the end the bees did leave, to find quieter homes. They found some other trunks to live in – hollow tree trunks!

CITY BEES
Sweet honey secrets to spot

Do you think that a busy city would be a good place for honey bees to live? The answer is yes! If there are trees and flowers growing around a town, we can make homes in hives there.

Can you find six beehives in the city? See if you can also spot:
* **someone watering a pot**
* **someone digging a garden**
* **a beekeeper looking after a hive**

City beekeepers often keep their hives dotted around town. They will visit the hives to look after them and collect honey.

City bees can live in hives on rooftops, in sheltered spots out of the wind.

Hooray for city bees!

The city bees can visit parks and gardens to gather pollen and nectar from trees and flowers, as well as flower pots that people put out on their balconies or window sills.

Bees will even find wild flowers in weedy, forgotten corners of town.

Bees like to visit vegetable gardens too. By pollinating the plants, bees help people in the city to grow fresh food.

THE BEEKEEPER COMES
Our careful, covered-up visitor

Once in a while we get a visit from someone who is dressed all in white, with her face behind a net. Our beekeeper has come to help us, but she must treat us gently or we might sting!

The beekeeper's jobs

The beekeeper must make sure we are all healthy in our hive.

In spring and autumn there might not be enough flower food for us to collect, so she gives us a sugary syrup to eat instead.

She takes away any extra honey that we have made and won't be eating.

She checks that our Queen is laying enough eggs. a our Queen is sick we might need a new one, and she can bring one for us.

The bee suit protects the beekeeper from bee stings.

The suit is white because it is a calming color for bees.

The sleeves are tight so bees won't get in.

The gloves are soft so that the beekeeper can handle the hive gently.

Smoke calms us down, so the beekeeper brings a smoker when she visits. It's a little metal container that has smoldering grass or wood chips inside. She uses it to puff smoke around our hive.

The beekeeper carries a soft bee brush to gently brush bees off the parts of the hive she is checking.

The beekeeper will take out honeycomb sections—called supers—from the hive, to drain out the honey.

The honey is in the comb.

The honey will get filtered to take out any unwanted bits and pieces, such as chunks of wax. Then it's ready to eat.

YUM!

WINTER SNUGGLE-UP
Furry huddles and snowdrop hunts

When winter snow blankets the meadow, it's too cold for us to fly. We huddle up inside our hive, waiting for days of soft sunshine.

We crowd together inside the hive, helping each other to stay warm.

We shiver and flap our wings to make heat.

Bumblebee Queens hibernate (sleep through winter) in a safe hiding place.

Shiver-shake, shiver-shake. The way to stay warm in winter!

We huddle around the Queen, taking turns moving to the middle or the outside.

Solitary bees lay eggs in safe places, so new bees will hatch in the spring.

We feed on the honey we made in the summer, or the sugary syrup that our beekeeper has put in the hive for us.

On warmer winter days we fly out to go to the toilet. This keeps our hive clean. Some of us will fly to find nectar and pollen in winter flowers, such as snowdrops.

Can you spot three little brown birds out in the snow?

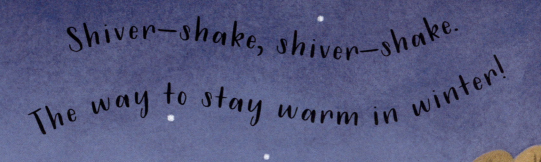

BE A BEE FRIEND
Recycle for us, plant for us, and dance with us

It's getting harder and harder to be a bee. We need flowers but we find them less and less. Some of the woods and meadows we fly over are disappearing too. Can you help?

Grow for the bees
You could grow some flowers that we like, in the ground or in a pot outside your home. Look for a packet of seeds marked as bee-friendly. We like flowers that are rich in nectar and pollen, such as sunflowers and lavender.

Check the seed packet for planting instructions.

The seeds will sprout and then flower, ready for the bees!

You could buy a bee-friendly plant that has already sprouted, such as a lavender.

Please don't pick wild flowers. Leave them for us to gather their goodness.

Throw for the bees
Have you heard of bee bombs? They are little balls of wild flower seeds mixed with soil and clay to keep them safe. If you throw a bee bomb on some cleared ground, the wild flowers might eventually bloom.

Build for the bees
If you have a garden, leave a little pile of scrap wood and sticks in a hidden corner. Bees and other insects can use it as shelter when they need to.

Us bees make the world a sweeter place, so don't forget to plant for us. You grow the seeds, the plants and, the trees, and we'll get busy buzzing around to give you back a world of flowers (and some golden honey for your spoon). See you soon!

Buzzwing the honey bee

My arms stretch out all day long.
I can be climbed,
but I'm not a mountain.
What am I?
I am Oakheart,
the oldest tree in the forest!

Dear Reader,

I do love riddles. After all, I am hundreds of years old and I know so very many of them. Did you know that I was born when people carried swords and galloped on horseback through the forest?

I have seen countless years bloom, flower, and fall, so I have a store of tree secrets to tell. A few of them are my own, such as how I was born, how I grew, and how I made my leaves. Others I have heard on the wind, and some were whispered to me by my friends the animals. They are very fond of magical stories and they have heard many on their travels. They know I love to hear them tell of tree wizards, dragons, and fairies as they nestle in my branches.

Read my book and one day, perhaps, your fingers will touch tree bark like mine and feel its lines, like a map of time. You will know the stories of my kind, and I hope you will help to care for us, little human. The knowledge of trees is my gift to you.

Oakheart the Brave

WHEN OAKHEART WAS BORN
A forgetful mouse and a lucky escape

I was once a seed hiding inside a tough brown coat—a tiny acorn sitting in a cup.

One day it was time for my parent tree to part with me, so I fell from its branch.

Some tree seeds are blown to other parts of the forest by the wind. Some are eaten by birds and fall later in their droppings. Me? I was stolen by a mouse!

As I lay on the ground, the mouse picked me up in her tiny paws and ran. Then *scribble, scrabble*, she dug a hole in the soil and hid me, thinking to come back and eat me later on. It was a close call. Luckily for me, my mouse wasn't the brightest furry beast in the forest, and she soon forgot all about me.

I was warm and cozy in my blanket of soil, and I had food with me inside my nut.

After a while I sent out a tiny root, very thin at first. It was a taproot that helped me to drink water and nutrients from the ground.

Then I sent out a shoot, up and up toward the warmth I could feel above me. Up and up I grew, through the grass and the leaves littering the forest floor, until at last I saw the sun.

I spread out my first tiny leaves.
One, two, then more.
I, Oakheart, was a tiny tree!

HOW TO FEED A TREE
A leafy recipe and some counting squirrels

What flutters but isn't a flag?
What falls but isn't water?
A leaf!
My leaves make me the food I need.

Oakheart's dinner recipe
(not for humans!)

If you want to make something yummy to eat you need a recipe. We trees have a recipe for our food, too, though it's not like yours. It's a kind of sugary mixture that helps us grow and stay alive. All the things we need to make it are in our leaves.

Ingredients

· **A green chemical called chlorophyll** (*clor-oh-fill*) It makes my leaves green and helps them to soak up sunlight.

· **A gas called carbon dioxide** My leaves soak it up from the air, through tiny holes called stomata (*stow-ma-ta*).

· **Water** It comes all the way up from my roots in the ground. Tiny veins carry it around inside my leaves.

My leaves use the carbon dioxide, the water, and sunlight soaked up by my chlorophyll to make sugary food. This mixes with more water and flows through my leaf veins. Any water that I don't need goes out through the stomata in my leaves into the air around me, along with a gas that I make called oxygen. That's a gas that you humans breathe. I'm glad I make some of it for you. Altogether, my food-making is called photosynthesis (*foe-toe-sin-the-sis*).

I am an old oak tree now. I think I have been alive for 500 years or so. Imagine! Every year since I grew tall I have made around 200,000 leaves. My friends the squirrels are good at numbers, and they worked out that I must have made about 100 million leaves altogether in my life. They asked me if I was tired, but I'll be fine for many more years, as long as I keep making my food.

MAGIC IN THE FOREST

A tree tale from Britain

A woodland wizard and some real magic

There are lots of old stories of tree magic. I think it's because forests seem to be mysterious places.

In Britain there is a legend from long ago about a mighty wizard named Merlin. He lived at the court of King Arthur and taught his magic to a clever woman named Nimue. But he didn't realize that she wanted to take his place, sitting at the side of the King.

Once Nimue was powerful enough, she waited for her chance to outwit Merlin. When the lords and ladies of the court went for a picnic in the forest one day, she tricked Merlin into getting lost in the woods. Then she used her magic to turn him into a tree!

The legend says that Merlin is sleeping in his tree, and one day he will wake, to help the world. Nimue is long gone, and so, though she tricked Merlin once, the forest has kept him safe and he will return one day.

On starlit nights I sometimes wonder if I have heard lords and ladies laughing and singing. I think I am dreaming, but even so I hope that you will agree that woods are definitely incredible places because of the things that really happen there. We trees use sunlight to make food, flowers, and fruit, and grow toward the sky. That's a kind of magic, isn't it!

WONDROUS FORESTS OF THE WORLD
What the wind told me

Sometimes the wind rustles through my branches, telling me about other forests full of astonishing trees and strange-sounding creatures. Perhaps when you are out in the world you will come across such places for yourself. I hope so. I wish you tree-luck, little traveler!

Rainforests grow in parts of the world where it is hot, steamy, and rainy all year-round. The rainforest trees are lush and tall, with vines hanging from them like jungle playground ropes. The Amazon Rainforest is the biggest. It stretches across Brazil in South America, and is home to many creatures.

Monkeys swing on vines between the trees.

Fir trees with sharp needles for leaves fill a huge forest that stretches for many miles across the far north of the world. It is called the **boreal forest**. In summer its ground is soft with bouncy green moss, or sometimes boggy and wet. In winter it is blanketed with snow and the creatures who live there leave their paw prints behind.

Big animals such as wild cats creep around looking for small animals to eat!

Small animals such as hares skitter around looking for plants to munch.

Butterflies the size of dinner plates flutter by.

Parrots zoom past, flashing rainbow wings.

The wind once told me about a special kind of rainforest called a **mangrove forest**. It grows in salty water along the edge of oceans. The mangrove tree roots snake into the water like a tangle of thick strings.

Birds are busy looking for food such as insects or seeds.

Wolves pad softly through the trees, on the hunt.

My own home is a **deciduous** (des-id-yew-us) **forest**. It grows in places that aren't very hot or cold. We have all sorts of different trees in our wood, but most of us drop our leaves in winter. The jungle trees in the rainforest and the fir trees in the boreal forest don't do that, so they are called evergreen.

HOW OAKHEART GREW
A little bit like you

Trees might grow slowly or quickly. They might stay short or reach up tall. They grow in different shapes. They're rather like people in that way, aren't they?

When I began I was just a stem, but every year I grew and grew, a little bit like you do.

My stem became my trunk. My branches became my crown, the part of me that spreads out.

By the time I was six I was taller than the top of anybody's head.

By the time I was 25 I was taller than a house with upstairs windows.

By the time I was 75 I was fully grown, as tall as an old ship with masts and sails. I was the maker of acorns and the home of animals.
I was Oakheart!

ROUGH AND WRINKLY
Tiny visitors and a too-tight coat

What has bark but no bite?
Me! A tree!

My bark is my skin. It's thicker and tougher than yours. It protects me from sun that could burn me and wind that could dry me out. I'll tell you all about it, and next time you see a big old tree like me, run your hand gently across its bark and whisper: "I know some secrets."

Tree bark can be smooth or wrinkly, scaly like snakeskin, papery, or even thorny. I heard that African kapok trees have bark covered in thorns as big as thumbs.

Why do I have lots of wrinkles and cracks in my bark? I got fatter! When a tree grows it pushes outward on its bark, as if it's bursting out of a coat that's too tight. The bark stretches and splits to give the tree more room.

I have some tree holes in my bark. They are places where branches have fallen off. I dropped some of my branches myself as I grew, and one or two have been blown off during fierce storms. I grew bark over the holes left behind.

Animals find shelter in my tree holes and bark cracks. Tiny spiders weave their webs. Beetles lay their eggs. Birds and mice pop in and out. I'm the big, helpful giant that gives them a home.

Not all animals are friendly visitors. Some insects could harm me with damage and disease. I have a trick to keep them away, though. I have natural chemicals in my bark that are poisonous to them.

I have outer bark, which is rough and wrinkly. Underneath I have inner bark, which is softer. The sugary food and water that I need runs around inside my inner bark.

SECRETS INSIDE US
Our clever layers and birthday rings

Inside your body you have all sorts of hidden things, such as bones and blood. We trees have hidden parts, too, but they are very different from yours. Ours are hidden in layers, like a sandwich. Let's look at tree layers together!

1. Where we are tough

Our outer bark is like a coat, the layer you can see. It protects us.

2. Where our food goes

Our inner bark is called the phloem (*flow-em*). The food we make travels around us through this layer, as sugary water called sap.

3. Where we get bigger

Next comes our growing layer, called the cambium (*cam-bee-um*). We make new wood in this part of us.

4. Where water gurgles upwards

Water and nutrients from the soil travel through a layer called the xylem (*zy-lem*). It goes all the way up from the ground to our leaves.

5. Where we are strongest

Our heartwood is a layer of dark wood around our middle. It's very strong and it holds us upright.

Every spring and summer I grow new layers of wood inside me. They look like the rings inside an onion.

In spring I grow fast, just like the flowers and baby chicks around me in the woods. My springwood is light in color.

In summer I take longer to grow. After all, when the sun is warm, who doesn't feel a little slow and lazy sometimes? My summerwood is dark in color.

If you ever find a slice of trunk from an old tree, you could try counting its rings to see how old it was. The different colored spring wood and summer wood means that there is a ring made every year. Counting is hard to do, though. There might be hundreds of rings!

ENEMIES!
Little critters, big dangers, and ways of winning

We trees have enemies,
little but deadly things
we don't want in our wood.
Wiggly fat caterpillars might
munch, munch on our leaves,
growing fatter.
Tunneling beetles might
chomp, chomp through our bark,
going deeper.
But we trees fight back.
We have ways of winning!

"Get ready for an attack, everyone. Make chemicals to protect yourselves!"

Some trees make chemicals and send a cloud of them into the air to warn their neighbors that they are being attacked. African umbrella acacia trees do this to warn their neighbors when hungry giraffes arrive to munch on them. The neighbors quickly make chemicals to turn their leaves bitter.

Some of us can make natural chemicals and put them into our leaves to make them taste bad to hungry animals. For instance, American green ash trees flood their leaves with chemicals to poison their enemy, the gypsy moth caterpillar.

"These leaves are yucky. I'm off!"

Some trees can send natural chemicals into the air to attract animals that will eat their enemies. Some apple trees are thought to do this to attract birds that eat leaf-killing caterpillars.

"Quickly, birds! Come and eat these pesky caterpillars!"

Pine trees make a sticky kind of syrup called resin. It has natural chemicals in it to keep enemies away. It can help to heal damage on the tree, too.

"My resin is like a bandage that I can put on myself."

TALLEST, OLDEST, BIGGEST, WIDEST

Some giraffes, elephants, buses, and me

Tiny Bird has flown to many wonderful places in the world. She has told me many things she has seen and heard about truly tremendous trees.

"You are tall, Oakheart, but you are not the tallest."

The tallest tree in the world is a coast redwood tree in the coastal forests of California, USA. It is called Hyperion, and it reaches up over 377 feet (115 m) tall. That's about as tall as a building with 26 storeys, or 20 big giraffes balanced on top of each other. Imagine that!

"You are heavy, Oakheart, but you are not the heaviest."

The heaviest tree is a giant sequoia in California. Its name is General Sherman and it weighs over 1,980 tons. That's about as much as 286 big African elephants. Imagine that!

"You are old, Oakheart, but you are not the oldest."

The oldest tree in the world is a bristlecone pine that grows in California. It is over 5,000 years old, so it has outlasted many kings and queens, emperors and chieftains. It was born about the time the wheel was invented. Imagine that!

"You are wide, Oakheart, but you are not the widest."

The widest tree in the world is a cypress tree in Oaxaca, Mexico. It's called El Árbol del Tule (the Tree of Tule), and it is almost 46 feet (14 m) wide. That's roughly as wide as five buses parked next to each other. Imagine that!

"But, my dear friend Oakheart... I think you are the kindest tree in the whole world. It's as if your heart is made of pure gold. Imagine that!"

THE WOODS IN SPRING
Blossom, buzzing, and some magic dust

The forest gets busy in springtime. The spring sun is our signal. When it bathes us in its warmth we trees begin to grow.

Buds are bursting. Leaves start unfurling from tiny buds on the tips of tree twigs.

Baby trees start sprouting up from seeds underground.

Below the trees, woodland **flowers bloom**, like colored sprinkles on the ground.

Bees are buzzing. You might hear them on their way to collect pollen and nectar from flowers. When they visit a flower they get sprinkled with pollen dust. The dust rubs off when they go to the next flower, helping it make new seeds.

Magic dust is in the air! The tree flowers make a powder called pollen. The **wind blows the pollen** to other trees, where it will settle on new flowers and help them make new seeds.

Birds are singing loudly to impress each other. They pair up to make nests, lay eggs and hatch their chicks.

Blossom flowers on the branches of trees. The flowers can be large or small. Some tiny tree flowers hang on catkins that look like furry tails.

THE FAIRY TREE

A tree tale from Scotland

A magical springtime journey

Feather Owl told me that long ago, in parts of Europe, spring was thought to be a magical time when you might come across the Queen of the Fairies. If you smelled the spring blossom of the hawthorn tree you might even travel to fairyland. This is an old, old story from Scotland about a man who did just that. He was named Thomas.

One spring day Thomas was sitting under a blossoming hawthorn tree, when he heard the sound of horse's hooves. A fair lady appeared before him on a white steed. She wore a silk dress and a golden velvet cloak. Her horse's mane was threaded with jingling silver bells.

Thomas had never seen such a beautiful lady. He knew that she must be a great queen, so he quickly knelt down. She smiled and asked him to come closer.

"If you sit behind me on my horse I will take you to Fairyland," she offered, so he did just that! The Queen spurred her horse to a gallop and off they went.

Soon they passed a red river.
   "This river is full of all the sadness on the Earth today," said the Queen.
   "Oh dear. There's so much!" gasped Thomas.
A little while later they passed a blue river.
   "This river is full of all the tears that have fallen on the Earth today," the Queen explained.
   "That's very sad. There are so many!" sighed Thomas.

At last they reached a beautiful orchard.
   "Welcome to Fairyland. Now I have a gift for you," said the Queen. She plucked an apple from a tree and handed it to Thomas, who by now was very hungry. When he bit into the juicy apple he was given the power to help other people, to lessen their sadness and stop their tears with his words.

The Queen took Thomas home. It seemed to him they had been gone for only one day, but he soon discovered that he had been gone for seven years! The Fairy Queen had given him a wonderful gift, but he had paid for it with time.

He became a great teacher and poet, helping people. They came from miles around to hear him speak, and they gave him the name Thomas the Rhymer. He never forgot the lesson he had learned from the Fairy Queen—you never know where you might go if you let your mind wander as you sit beneath a blossoming hawthorn tree. Be prepared to dream great things, but also to lose some time...

THE WOODS IN SUMMER
Spreading, hatching, fluttering, zooming

In summer the woods are a shady, cool, green hideaway—but there is still lots going on...

There's **a leafy roof** in early summer, as trees are busy growing. Their leaves spread like a shady green ceiling over the woods.

The air is **busy with minibeasts.** You might see flying insects such as midges and dragonflies zooming through shafts of sunlight beneath the trees.

In late summer, when trees stop growing, they begin **storing food** in their roots. They will need the stores of food over the winter and in spring when it's time to start growing again.

THE SUMMER STORM

A tree tale from Norway

An angry boy and a clever bear

Sometimes the heat of summer brings on summer lightning storms. One summer storm was the reason I got my nickname—Oakheart the Brave. I wasn't really brave, I don't think, though my friends insisted I was. I just did what we trees are good at doing —giving shelter to creatures smaller than us.

One evening a summer storm came to the woods. Roll! CRACK! Thunder and lightning crashed and flashed above us. "It's so noisy and scary!" cried the squirrels, the birds, and the mice living in my branches, so I thought of a way to help them. "I'll tell you a story," I said. "Listen to my words very carefully, not to the sound of the storm."

Long ago, in a land of legend, there was a fearsome Viking god called Thor. Whenever he lost his temper he made thunder and lightning by swinging his giant hammer.

One summer evening, when Thor was still a boy, the other Viking gods teased him and made him angry. He stomped across the sky, swinging his hammer and making a terrible stormy racket.

Down below, a mother bear and her two cubs were woken from a nap in their forest home.
"Hey, Thor. Why are you being so noisy?" Mother Bear cried.
"I'm upset. I got teased!" barked Thor.
"Come and be with us. We won't be mean," said Mother Bear, so Thor came down to the forest and, sure enough, he found some kind friends. He played hide-and-seek with the bears and they showed him where to find delicious forest honey and sweet stream water.

Thor had such fun that he forgot to be bad-tempered and the storm ended. For Mother Bear knew an important secret—kindness sends away anger.

When my story about Thor was done, so was the summer storm over our wood. "Thank you, Oakheart. That was very kind of you. Listening to you made us feel much better," cried the squirrels.
"You weren't scared. You were so brave," added the mice. "Oakheart the Brave! Oakheart the Brave!"
I wasn't all that brave, really. I was just making sure I helped other living things, because that way everyone is happier. I suppose that's an important secret, too!

THE WOODS IN AUTUMN
Falling leaves, juicy fruit and flying flocks

In autumn the woods change in lots of ways. The trees are getting ready for the winter to come.

Lots of **trees lose their leaves** in autumn. They don't need them for making food anymore. They will grow new leaves next spring.

Leaves are changing color. Before leaves fall they start to look orange, yellow, or red instead of green. This is because the natural chemicals inside them change.

Fallen **leaves make a good home** for beetles, bugs, and all kinds of creatures on the forest floor.

The leaves that fall **help the soil** by rotting down and adding nutrients.

It's **time for some birds to fly** off to warmer places for the winter. They often travel together in a flock. Some of my bird friends will stay, though, and a few will even arrive from colder parts of the world to spend the winter with me.

Many **trees make fruit** at this time of year. When the fruit drops to the ground the seeds inside will go into the soil, ready to grow as new plants in spring.

All sorts of **fungi grow** in the autumn wood, in lots of sizes and shapes. There are fungi shaped like plates, cups, hats, or even footballs.

Don't touch fungi. Some of them are poisonous! Leave them for animals such as slugs, who can safely nibble on them.

Autumn is the time for fungi to spread their tiny seedlike spores on the wind. The spores will one day grow into new fungi.

THE TREE OF LIFE

A tree tale from Persia

Invisible fruit and a hidden dragon

In the autumn Feather Owl likes to tell me this fruit story from long ago. She says that in many countries there are legends about a fabulous tree called the Tree of Life. In Ancient Persia the tree was said to have one of every fruit in the world hanging from its branches, but there was a catch: the fruit was invisible!

The Tree of Life was very precious. If any of its fruit got damaged, that kind of fruit would disappear from the world forever. Because of this it was guarded by a dragon named Simarghu, but he was invisible too.

Nobody knew which tree in Persia was the Tree of Life, or where the invisible dragon might be, so no one dared go into the forests at all…Nobody, that is, except for a girl who forgot about the story one day—she was too busy following a beautiful butterfly. She followed it into the woods near her home, then sat down on a long tree root to watch it.

The root seemed to shiver and then stir. It turned into Simarghu the dragon, who was curled around a tree trunk.

"Oh! Aren't you meant to be invisible?" cried the girl, jumping up in surprise.

"I'll be whatever I like, thank you very much," snapped the grumpy dragon.

The girl looked up and saw one of every fruit in the world hanging from the branches of the tree above her head. Without thinking, she reached out to pick a juicy-looking peach.

"Wait! Tell me something. Are you hungry?" cried Simarghu.

"Not really," admitted the girl.

"Then are you thirsty?" he asked.

"Er...No," admitted the girl.

"If you take that peach, then all peaches will disappear from the world forever," said Simarghu. "I won't stop you, though. You decide for yourself."

The girl bowed her head and thrust her hands deeply in her pockets.

"I'm sorry. I won't take anything. It would be very selfish," she replied. When she looked up again the fruit and the dragon were gone, and all the trees around her looked the same.

The girl returned home, but she never forgot what she had learned. As soon as she was able, she wove a beautiful Persian carpet that showed the magical tree. Anyone who stepped on it was reminded to tread carefully across our precious planet and do no harm.

The carpet's message was this: "Look after the woods of the world. Let Simarghu the dragon sleep in peace and let the Tree of Life survive."

THE WOODS IN WINTER
Sleepy bats and snowy tracks

In winter woodlands, we trees have a rest. The woods are a peaceful place, and some of our animal friends are sleeping, too. Even so, there is still lots to see.

Trees are sleeping or dormant, which means they do not make food or grow new wood.

Many trees are still green. **Evergreen conifer** trees keep their needle leaves. The needles have a waxy coating to protect them from losing too much water when the ground is frozen.

There are **secret homes** to see. You can spot empty bird's nests perched up in the bare tree branches. They would usually be hidden by leaves.

Someone is taking a long nap. Animals, such as bats, hibernate in winter. They have a long sleep and save their energy for spring.

Other animals are out and about. Birds hop around looking for food. It can be tough finding something to eat when there is lots of snow and ice.

Frogs, toads, snakes, lizards, bumblebees, and bears are all woodland animals that **rest during the winter.**

Animals leave tracks. You might see woodland animal footprints in the winter snow. Look out for the print of a deer hoof. It looks like two tiny eyes and two long bunny ears.

Baby bears are born in winter in North America, hidden away inside a safe den with their mom. At first, they are tiny, about as long as a banana. They will drink their mother's milk and grow, ready to peek outside for the first time in spring.

TREES MADE THESE
Pirate ships and palaces, poems and paper

We trees don't live forever, but don't be sad. We don't disappear! Our wood can make wonderful things.

Trees made...

Tall ships that sailed the world, with hulls curved like whale bellies. Sailors and fishermen, explorers and pirates, all skimmed the waves in these wooden sea nests.

Trees made...

The mighty halls of kings and queens, with roof beams like giants' fingers. Rulers, wizards, and warrior heroes all feasted in these wooden strongholds.

Trees made...

The pencils, easels, chairs, and desks used by storymakers, poets, and artists, busy writing and drawing their dreams.

Trees made...

Some stairs, a door, a floor, a bed, where someone is snuggling, reading this book, made of paper, made of wood!

Even if our wood is not used to make new things, our fallen logs provide a home for many little animals in the forest. Eventually the wood crumbles into the soil, adding nutrients and helping to make it rich.

Hopefully, new tree shoots start to grow in the space the old trees leave behind.

HOW TO BE TREE-HAPPY

Recycle us, plant us, and dance with us

There are things that you can do to help
us trees and yourself, too.

Make sure you recycle

Things that are made of wood, such as paper and cardboard,
can be recycled. That way they won't go to waste.

Be a tree friend

Be careful not to damage trees by breaking open bark
or pulling down branches, and make sure you
don't leave litter behind when you visit us.

Grow new trees

Find out how to help plant new trees
where you live. You could even collect some
seeds and try growing some yourself.

1. You can grow oaks from tiny acorns. Choose a plump brown one (green ones are not ripe and black ones are too ripe).

2. Plant the acorn, pointed end upwards, about 1 inch (2.5 cm) down in a yogurt tub full of soil. Put the tub in a cool place out of scorching sunlight. A shelf in a garage or a shed is a good place.

3. Your acorn should sprout in four to six weeks. Put it somewhere sunny and give it a little water every couple of weeks (not too much). Put it in a bigger pot when it is about the length of a banana.

4. Eventually, when the seedling is about as tall as this book, you can plant it outside. Choose somewhere where it will have room to grow big and tall one day. It will take many years, but good things are worth the wait.

Sit with trees,
walk through trees,
talk to trees,
and definitely
dance with trees.

We trees need you to care for us,
and in return we hope you have a lovely
time when you visit.

Oh… and remember to call out a "Hello"
next time you are in a wood.
Who knows? I might be growing nearby…
See you soon!

Oakheart the Brave

© 2025 Quarto Publishing Group USA Inc.
Text © 2025 Moira Butterfield
Illustrations © 2025 Vivian Mineker Chen

Moira Butterfield has asserted her right
to be identified as the author of this work.
Vivian Mineker Chen has asserted her right
to be identified as the illustrator of this work.

Senior Designer: Sarah Chapman-Suire
Editors: Victoria Garrard, Sarah Higgins,
Carly Madden, Emily Pither, and Harriet Stone
Consultants: Michael Bright, John House,
and Kevin Warwick
Creative Director: Malena Stojic
Associate Publisher: Rhiannon Findlay
Production Manager: Nikki Ingram

First published as The Secret Life of Bugs in 2024.
First published as The Secret Life of Bees in 2021.
First published as The Secret Life of Trees in 2020.

This bind-up edition published in 2025
by Happy Yak, an imprint of The Quarto Group.
100 Cummings Center, Suite 265D,
Beverly, MA 01915, USA.
T (978) 282-9590 F (978) 283-2742
www.quarto.com

All rights reserved. No part of this publication
may be reproduced, stored in a retrieval system,
or transmitted in any form, or by any means,
electrical, mechanical, photocopying, recording,
or otherwise, without the prior written permission
of the publisher or a license permitting
restricted copying.

ISBN 978 1 83600 370 0

Manufactured in Guangdong, China TT012025
9 8 7 6 5 4 3 2 1